*A*DVENT *and*
*C*HRISTMAS
*W*ISDOM
from
SAINT FRANCIS OF ASSISI

$\mathscr{A}$DVENT and $\mathscr{C}$HRISTMAS $\mathscr{W}$ISDOM

—— *from* ——

SAINT FRANCIS
OF ASSISI

Daily Scripture and Prayers
Together With
Saint Francis of Assisi's Own Words

Compiled by John V. Kruse, PhD

Liguori
LIGUORI, MISSOURI

Imprimi Potest:
Thomas D. Picton, C.Ss.R.
Provincial, Denver Province
The Redemptorists

Published by Liguori
Liguori, Missouri
To order, call 800-325-9521
www.liguori.org

Library of Congress Cataloging-in-Publication Data

Advent and Christmas wisdom from Saint Francis of Assisi : daily Scripture and prayers together with Saint Francis of Assisi's own words /compiled by John V. Kruse. — 1st ed.
    p. cm.
    ISBN 978-0-7648-1756-4
    1. Advent—Prayers and devotions. 2. Christmas—Prayers and devotions. 3. Catholic Church—Prayers and devotions. I. Francis, of Assisi, Saint, 1182-1226. II. Kruse, John V.
BX2170.A4A36 2008
242'.33—dc22

                                                        2008027352

Printed in the United States of America
12 11 10 09   5 4 3 2

Contents

Epigraph

"I RETURN FROM PERUGIA and arrive here in the dead of night. It's wintertime, muddy, and so cold that icicles have formed on the edges of my habit and keep striking my legs and blood flows from such wounds. Freezing, covered with mud and ice, I come to the gate and, after I've knocked and called for some time, a brother comes and asks: 'Who are you?' 'Brother Francis,' I answer. "Go away!' he says. 'This is not a decent hour to be wandering about! You may not come in!' When I insist, he replies: 'Go away! You are simple and stupid! Don't come back to us again! There are many of us here like you—we don't need you!' I stand again at the door and say: 'For the love of God, take me in tonight!' And he replies: 'I will not! Go to the Crosiers' place and ask there!'

"I tell you this: If I had patience and did not become upset, true joy, as well as true virtue and the salvation of my soul, would consist in this."

SAINT FRANCIS' RESPONSE TO THE QUESTION, "WHAT IS TRUE JOY?" AS WRITTEN IN A LETTER TO BROTHER LEO, "TRUE AND PERFECT JOY," 166-167.

Introduction

SAINT FRANCIS OF ASSISI (1181/2-1226) abandoned the comfortable life of the medieval Italian merchant class to embrace a life of radical Christian discipleship as he interpreted it being depicted in the gospels. Christ's birth greatly influenced Francis' understanding of what it meant to be a follower of Christ. For Francis, to live the life of a disciple of Christ meant that one had to embrace the poverty and humility of Christ as made manifest in Christ's own birth.

In *The Life of Saint Francis* (1229), the first account of the life of Saint Francis to be written, Brother Thomas of Celano describes Francis as having created a live nativity scene in the town of Greccio, Italy, three years prior to the saint's death. Francis desired to enter into the sights, smells, and sounds of the scene so that he could gain a more accurate sense of the real significance of the birth of Christ. Through the experience of this first known nativity scene, Francis was especially moved by the simplicity, humility, and poverty of the scene. There in this "new Bethlehem," Francis could grapple with how the infinite God, in an unfathomable act of love, had taken on our human condition as a vulnerable baby born amidst animals and laid in a manger.

When we turn to the writings of Francis himself, some that were actually written by the saint's own hand, others that were transcribed by his followers, we come across many themes that are especially appropriate for the Advent and Christmas seasons. For example, Francis speaks of humility, love, joy, patience, hospitality, peace, gratitude, and openness to the will of God. Francis also speaks of poverty, which is especially important in that Francis believed that the Christ who had humbled himself by being born in the impoverished environment of a stable continues to be found amongst the poor and disenfranchised of our own world. May Francis' own words lead all of us to the wondrous miracle of the manger.

How to Use This Book

Advent—that period of great anticipatory joy—is a time of preparation for the celebration of Christ's arrival in Bethlehem as a helpless infant. In the Western liturgy, Advent begins four Sundays prior to December 25—the Sunday closest to November 30, which is the feast of Saint Andrew, one of Jesus' first disciples.

The annual commemoration of Christ's birth begins the Christmas cycle of the liturgical year—a cycle that runs from Christmas Eve to the Sunday after the feast of the Epiphany. In keeping with the unfolding of the message of the liturgical year, this book is designed to be used during the entire period from the first Sunday of Advent to the end of the Christmas cycle.

The four weeks of Advent are often thought of as symbolizing the four different ways that Christ comes into the world: (1) at his birth as a helpless infant in Bethlehem; (2) at his arrival in the hearts of believers; (3) at his death; and (4) at his arrival on Judgment Day.

Because Christmas falls on a different day of the week each year, the fourth week of Advent is never really finished; it is abruptly, joyously, and solemnly abrogated by the annual coming again of Christ at Christmas. Christ's Second Coming will also one day abruptly interrupt our sojourn here on earth.

Since the calendar dictates the number of days in Advent, this book includes Scripture quotations and meditative excerpts from the writings of Saint Francis of Assisi for a full twenty-eight days. These twenty-eight daily readings make up Part I of this book. It is suggested that the reader begin at the beginning and, on Christmas Day, switch to Part II, which contains materials for the twelve days of Christmas. If there are any "extra" entries from Part I, these may be read by doubling up days, if so desired, or by reading two entries on weekends. Alternately, one may just skip those entries that do not fit within the Advent time frame for that particular year.

Each "day" in this book begins with the words of Saint Francis of Assisi. Following that quotation is an excerpt from Scripture, which is related in some way to the beginning quote. Next is provided a small prayer, also built on the ideas from the two preceding passages. Finally, an Advent or Christmas activity is suggested as a way to apply the messages to one's daily life.

PART I

~~~~~~

READINGS FOR ADVENT

DAY 1

The Will of God

Most High,
glorious God,
enlighten the darkness of my heart
and give me
true faith,
certain hope,
and perfect charity,
sense and knowledge,
Lord,
that I may carry out
Your holy and true command.

SAINT FRANCIS OF ASSISI,
"THE PRAYER BEFORE THE CRUCIFIX," 40

LET IT BE

The angel said to her, "Do not be afraid, Mary, for you have found favor with God. And now, you will conceive in your womb and bear a son, and you will name him Jesus. ...Mary said to the angel, "How can this be, since I am a virgin?" The angel said to her, "The Holy Spirit will come upon you, and the power of the Most High will overshadow you; therefore the child to be born will be holy; he will be called Son of God. And now, your relative Elizabeth in her old age has also conceived a son; and this is the sixth month for her who was said to be barren. For nothing will be impossible with God." Then Mary said, "Here am I, the servant of the Lord; let it be with me according to your word." Then the angel departed from her.

LUKE 1:30-31, 34-38

PRAYER

Lord, being a Christian means that I am called to live a life that involves a degree of uncertainty. Like Mary, I am unsure what your call will require of me in the next moment, tomorrow, or many years from now. Strengthen my trust in you so that I may be your faithful servant in the world.

ADVENT ACTION

We are often surrounded with much noise that drowns out the voice of God in our lives. Create an environment in which to listen to God speaking to you, so that you may better follow his will in your life. When in the car or when in your home, allow yourself a period of silence by not turning on the radio, stereo, or television.

DAY 2

Growing in the Virtue of Patience

*W*here there is patience and humility,
There is neither anger nor disturbance.

SAINT FRANCIS OF ASSISI, *THE ADMONITIONS*
(XXVII: VIRTUE PUTS VICE TO FLIGHT), 136

...[L]et them [the brothers] pay attention to what they must desire above all else: to have the Spirit of the Lord and Its holy activity, to pray always to Him with a pure heart, to have humility and patience in persecution and infirmity...

SAINT FRANCIS OF ASSISI, *THE LATER RULE*
(X: THE ADMONITION AND CORRECTION OF THE BROTHERS), 105

WAITING WITH PATIENCE FOR THE LORD

Be patient, therefore, beloved, until the coming of the Lord. The farmer waits for the precious crop from the earth, being patient with it until it receives the early and the late rains. You also must be patient. Strengthen your hearts, for the coming of the Lord is near.

JAMES 5:7-8

PRAYER

Lord of all longing, in our society of instant gratification, patience is not a cultivated virtue. Remind me that I do not need to immediately have all the things I long for and all the answers to my questions. In the waiting, we often learn much about ourselves, come to a greater awareness of what is truly important in life, and gain a better appreciation for the things we must await.

ADVENT ACTION

When someone or some circumstance causes you to wait today, slow down and view that person or circumstance as a blessing. Is it really that important that you immediately have what you want? What do you learn about yourself as you wait? What do you notice around you when you slow down to wait?

DAY 3

The Humility of God in the Incarnation

*T*he most high Father made known from heaven through His holy angel Gabriel this Word of the Father—so worthy, so holy and glorious—in the womb of the glorious Virgin Mary, from whose womb He received the flesh of our humanity and frailty. Though He was rich, He wished, together with the most Blessed Virgin, His mother, to choose poverty in the world beyond all else.

2 Cor 8:9

SAINT FRANCIS OF ASSISI,
"LATER ADMONITION AND EXHORTATION
TO THE BROTHERS AND SISTERS OF PENANCE," 46

CHRIST'S HUMILITY

Let the same mind be in you that was in Christ Jesus,
who, though he was in the form of God,
did not regard equality with God
as something to be exploited,
but emptied himself,
taking the form of a slave,
being born in human likeness.
And being found in human form,
he humbled himself
and became obedient to the point of death—
even death on a cross.

PHILIPPIANS 2:5-8

PRAYER

Humble God, in your humility, you reached out to the human race in order to draw us into a communion that could not have been possible through any other means. May Jesus be a friend who can identify with all that we go through in life, who brings us into a relationship with his Father, and who, by his humility and self-sacrificing love, shows us what it means to live human life to its fullest.

ADVENT ACTION

Take time to reflect on the significance of what it means that God took on human flesh to share himself with us. As you move through your day, with all of its ups and downs, remember that Christ can truly identify with all that you experience because of the humility of the Incarnation.

DAY 4

The Simplicity of Poverty

*W*hen the brothers go through the world, let them take *nothing* for the journey, *neither knapsack, nor purse, nor bread, nor money, nor walking stick. Whatever house they enter,* let them first say: Peace to this house. They may eat and drink *what is placed before them* for as long as they stay *in that house.* [...] *Whoever takes their cloak, let them not withhold their tunic. Let them give to all who ask of them and whoever takes what is theirs, let them not seek to take it back.*

Lk 9:3;
Lk 10:4;
Mt 10:10

Lk 10:5

Lk 10:7

Lk 6:29

Lk 6:30

SAINT FRANCIS OF ASSISI, *THE EARLIER RULE*,
(XIV: HOW THE BROTHERS SHOULD GO THROUGH THE WORLD), 73*

Passages taken from the Scripture are in italics.

LEAVING ALL TO FOLLOW JESUS

A certain ruler asked him, "Good Teacher, what must I do to inherit eternal life?" Jesus said to him, "… You know the commandments: 'You shall not commit adultery; You shall not murder; You shall not steal; You shall not bear false witness; Honor your father and mother.' "He replied, "I have kept all these since my youth." When Jesus heard this, he said to him, "There is still one thing lacking. Sell all that you own and distribute the money to the poor, and you will have treasure in heaven; then come, follow me." But when he heard this, he became sad; for he was very rich.

LUKE 18:18-23

PRAYER

Lord of all simplicity, so many people have made getting *things* the focus of this season of your birth. Material things are only good to the degree that they help us grow in our relationship with you. Help us learn from the example of Francis: the less we have, the less we have to worry about and the more we can keep a focus on what is really important—you.

ADVENT ACTION

Can't think of what to buy for the friend or loved one who has everything? Instead of purchasing something, let that special person know how much he or she means to you in a card or letter.

DAY 5

Forgiveness

Forgive us our trespasses   Mt 6:12
through Your ineffable mercy
through the power of the passion of Your beloved Son
and through the merits and intercession of the ever
blessed Virgin and all Your elect.

As we forgive those who trespass against us   Mt 6:12
And what we do not completely forgive,
make us, Lord, forgive completely
that we may truly love our enemies because of You
and we may fervently intercede for them before You,
returning no evil for evil   1 Thes 5:15
and may we strive to help everyone in You.

SAINT FRANCIS OF ASSISI,
"A PRAYER INSPIRED BY THE OUR FATHER," 159

FORGIVING AS GOD FORGIVES

As God's chosen ones, holy and beloved, clothe yourselves with compassion, kindness, humility, meekness, and patience. Bear with one another and, if anyone has a complaint against another, forgive each other; just as the Lord has forgiven you, so you also must forgive. Above all, clothe yourselves with love, which binds everything together in perfect harmony. And let the peace of Christ rule in your hearts, to which indeed you were called in the one body. And be thankful.

COLOSSIANS 3:12-15

PRAYER

Forgiving God, the expectations and pressures that often accompany this holy season sometimes lead old hurts and grudges to surface and new ones to appear. Letting go of hurts can be one of the most difficult things to do in life. May I seek to forgive as you forgive, for in forgiveness comes healing.

ADVENT ACTION

Forgiving doesn't necessarily mean forgetting, but it does mean letting go of the grudge and animosity that you hold over another. What relationship in your life is in need of healing? Let go of a grudge today and do something concrete to extend a hand of reconciliation.

DAY 6

Hospitality

*W*herever the brothers may be, either in hermitages or other places, let them be careful not to make any place their own or contend with anyone for it. Whoever comes to them, friend or foe, thief or robber, let him be received with kindness.

SAINT FRANCIS, *THE EARLIER RULE*,
(VII: THE MANNER OF SERVING AND WORKING), 69

MAKING ROOM FOR CHRIST
BY MAKING ROOM FOR OTHERS

And she gave birth to her firstborn son and wrapped him in bands of cloth, and laid him in a manger, because there was no place for them in the inn.

LUKE 2:7

PRAYER

Lord, in our world, many people feel unwelcome and excluded, whether because of race, a mental or physical condition, ethnicity, social-economic level, or simply because they are "different." It seems as if our world has no room for such people. Help me to see your face in such people, for when I make strangers and the socially outcast feel welcome, I am, in fact, welcoming you.

ADVENT ACTION

Reach out and make an effort to include someone who might feel excluded or "pushed to the side." Offer a kind word or a word of welcome to this person. Include someone in a social function or conversation who might otherwise be forgotten.

DAY 7

The Power of Words

*L*et all the brothers be careful not to slander or engage in disputes; let them strive, instead, to keep silence whenever 2 Tm 2:14 God gives them the grace. Let them not quarrel among themselves or with others but strive to respond humbly, saying: *I am a useless* servant.... Lk 17:10

Let them revile no one. Let them not grumble or detract from Ti 3:2 others, for it is written: *Gossips* and *detractors* are *detestable* to Rom 1:29-30 God. Let them be *modest by showing graciousness toward everyone.* Let them not judge or condemn. Ti 3:2

SAINT FRANCIS OF ASSISI, *THE EARLIER RULE*,
(XI: THE BROTHERS SHOULD NOT REVILE OR DETRACT,
BUT SHOULD LOVE ONE ANOTHER), 72

PROPER USE OF THE TONGUE

Rash words are like sword thrusts,
but the tongue of the wise brings healing.
Truthful lips endure for ever,
but a lying tongue lasts only a moment.

PROVERBS 12:18-19

PRAYER

Word Made Flesh, I can use my tongue to build up or to tear down. Give me the gift of your wisdom so that I might choose my words wisely and know when it is best to hold my tongue. May my words encourage, inspire, and heal, rather than wound.

ADVENT ACTIVITY

Practice the art of holding your tongue. Make a conscious effort to think before you speak. When tempted to make a biting comment, instead say nothing. Let someone else have the last word in a conversation, argument, or disagreement.

DAY 8

Caring for One Another

Let each one confidently make known his need to another that the other might discover what is needed and minister to him. Let each one love and care for his brother as a mother loves and cares for her son in those matters in which God has given him the grace.

SAINT FRANCIS OF ASSISI, *THE EARLIER RULE*,
(IX: BEGGING ALMS), 71

CHRISTIAN CARE

All who believed were together and had all things in common; they would sell their possessions and goods and distribute the proceeds to all, as any had need. Day by day, as they spent much time together in the temple, they broke bread at home and ate their food with glad and generous hearts, praising God and having the goodwill of all the people. And day by day the Lord added to their number those who were being saved.

ACTS 2:44-47

PRAYER

Lord, during this hectic season, I often become so absorbed in my own little world that I am not attentive to the needs of others. Help me to express my own needs humbly and to meet the needs of others graciously. By doing so, may I be drawn into a closer relationship with others and with you.

ADVENT ACTIVITY

Let a friend or loved one know of a personal need and give him or her the opportunity to be of service to you. Take time to ask a friend, co-worker, or family member how you could assist him or her today.

DAY 9

In Praise of God's Goodness

*A*ll-powerful, most holy, most high, supreme God: all good, supreme good, totally good, You Who *alone are good*, may we give You all praise, all *glory*, all thanks, all *honor*, all *blessing*, and all good. So be it! So be it! Amen.

Lk 18:19

Rv 5:12

SAINT FRANCIS OF ASSISI,
"THE PRAISES TO BE SAID AT ALL HOURS," 162

PRAISING THE LORD'S POWER AND GOODNESS

For the Lord your God is God of gods and Lord of lords, the great God, mighty and awesome. …You shall fear the Lord your God; him alone you shall worship; to him you shall hold fast, and by his name you shall swear. He is your praise; he is your God, who has done for you these great and awesome things that your own eyes have seen. Your ancestors went down to Egypt seventy persons; and now the Lord your God has made you as numerous as the stars in heaven.

DEUTERONOMY 10:17, 20-22

PRAYER

Almighty God, in this season in which you performed your most wondrous work of assuming human flesh, my heart stirs as I lift up my voice in humble praise of your goodness and greatness: I praise you, O Lord!

ADVENT ACTIVITY

On a slip of paper, write out, "I praise you, O Lord, for …" and list three things for which you praise God. Use the paper as a bookmark in this book during these seasons of Advent and Christmas.

Gratitude

All-powerful, most holy,
Almighty and supreme God,
Holy and just *Father,*   Jn 17:11
Lord King *of heaven and earth*   Mt 11:25
We thank You for Yourself
for through Your holy will
and through Your only Son
with the Holy Spirit
You have created everything spiritual and corporal
and, after making us *in Your own image and likeness,*
You placed us in paradise.   Gn 1:26; 2:15

      SAINT FRANCIS OF ASSISI, *THE EARLIER RULE,*
      (XXIII: PRAYER AND THANKSGIVING), 81-82

GIVE THANKS TO THE LORD FOR ALL HE HAS GIVEN US

O give thanks to the Lord, call on his name,
   make known his deeds among the peoples.
Sing to him, sing praises to him;
   tell of all his wonderful works.
Glory in his holy name;
   let the hearts of those who seek the Lord rejoice.
Seek the Lord and his strength;
   seek his presence continually.
Remember the wonderful works he has done,
   his miracles, and the judgements he has uttered…

PSALM 105:1-5

PRAYER

Gracious God, there are many gifts which you have given me: your Son who came to dwell among us, creation, my friends and family, my very life, and all that sustains me. Those around me serve as channels of your goodness and offer me much for which to be grateful. All that I have is a blessing.

ADVENT ACTION

Is there someone in your life whom you have recently taken for granted? Express a word of gratitude telling that person all that he or she means to you.

≈≈≈≈ **DAY 11** ≈≈≈≈≈≈≈≈≈≈≈≈≈≈≈≈≈≈≈≈

Courtesy and Respect

I counsel, admonish and exhort my brothers in the Lord
Jesus Christ not to quarrel or argue or judge others when 2 Tm 2:14
they go about in the world; but let them be meek, peaceful,
modest, gentle, and humble, speaking courteously to everyone,
as is becoming.

SAINT FRANCIS OF ASSISI, *THE LATER RULE*,
(III: THE DIVINE OFFICE, FASTING, AND
HOW THE BROTHERS SHOULD GO ABOUT IN THE WORLD), 102

Treating Others As You Would Be Treated

"In everything do to others as you would have them do to you; for this is the law and the prophets."

MATTHEW 7:12

Prayer

Lord, help me to step outside of myself, to be aware of those around me, and to demonstrate care and respect for others. Let me treat all people as I would like to be treated. All people are made in your image and likeness, and by respecting them, I also show respect for you.

Advent Action

Offer a word of kindness and acknowledge the dignity of those you pass on the street or meet in the elevator. Do the same for those who work in what are often thankless jobs, for example, food service, retail, and housekeeping.

DAY 12

Being Content with the Blessings God Has Given Us

...[W]hoever envies his brother the good that the Lord says or does in him incurs the sin of blasphemy because he envies the Most High Himself Who says and does every good thing. _{Mt 20:15}

SAINT FRANCIS OF ASSISI, *THE ADMONITIONS*,
(VIII: AVOIDING THE SIN OF ENVY), 132

THE GIFT THAT COMES WITH LETTING GO OF ENVY

For where there is envy and selfish ambition, there will also be disorder and wickedness of every kind. But the wisdom from above is first pure, then peaceable, gentle, willing to yield, full of mercy and good fruits, without a trace of partiality or hypocrisy. And a harvest of righteousness is sown in peace for those who make peace.

JAMES 3:16-18

PRAYER

My God and my All, envy can become a force that blinds and consumes me, and I don't want to be any person other than whom you made me. Calling me your daughter or son is a gift that comes from you alone. May my Advent experience deepen as I look at my sisters and brothers with the eyes of faith and not the eyes of envy.

ADVENT ACTION

Of what are you envious? Consider what it is that you really need and value in your life. Rejoice in the good fortune of another and say a prayer for someone whose situation may seem idyllic, but which in reality and unbeknownst to you, may be a cause of pain and suffering for that person.

DAY 13

Performing Acts of Penance

*A*ll those who love the Lord *with their whole heart, with their whole soul and mind, with their whole strength* and love their neighbors as themselves...who receive the Body and Blood of our Lord Jesus Christ, and who produce worthy fruits of penance. O how happy and blessed are these men and women while they do such things and persevere in doing them, because *the Spirit of the Lord will rest upon them* and *make* Its home and *dwelling place* among them, and they are children of the heavenly Father Whose works they do.... Mk 12:30 Mt 22:39 Is 11:2 Jn 14:23 Mt 5:45

SAINT FRANCIS OF ASSISI, *EARLIER EXHORTATION TO THE BROTHERS AND SISTERS OF PENANCE*, (I : THOSE WHO DO PENANCE), 41-42

PROPER PENANCE AND FASTING

"And whenever you fast, do not look dismal, like the hypocrites, for they disfigure their faces so as to show others that they are fasting. Truly I tell you, they have received their reward. But when you fast, put oil on your head and wash your face, so that your fasting may be seen not by others but by your Father who is in secret; and your Father who sees in secret will reward you.

MATTHEW 6:16-18

PRAYER

Lord of mercy and kindness, during this season of patient waiting, may works of penance not gain me the attention and praise of others, but deepen my awareness that your kingdom comes through forgiveness. Inspired by the hopefulness of this season, I ask you to pick me up and lead me back to a more faithful relationship with you.

ADVENT ACTION

Take time to perform a serious examination of conscience. In what areas of your relationship with God are you falling short? What improvements can you make? Celebrate the Sacrament of Reconciliation this Advent season.

Sharing Our Gifts

*L*et us, therefore, have charity and humility and give alms because it washes the stains of sins from our souls. For, _{Tb 4:11; 12:9} although people lose everything they leave behind in this world, they, nevertheless, carry with them the rewards of charity and the alms they have given for which they will receive a reward and a fitting repayment from the Lord.

SAINT FRANCIS OF ASSISI,
"LATER ADMONITION AND EXHORTATION
TO THE BROTHERS AND SISTERS OF PENANCE" 47

SHARING OUTSIDE OF OUR COMFORT ZONES

He [Jesus] sat down opposite the treasury, and watched the crowd putting money into the treasury. Many rich people put in large sums. A poor widow came and put in two small copper coins, which are worth a penny. Then he called his disciples and said to them, "Truly I tell you, this poor widow has put in more than all those who are contributing to the treasury. For all of them have contributed out of their abundance; but she out of her poverty has put in everything she had, all she had to live on."

MARK 12:41-44

PRAYER

Lord, our society often seems to be abounding in excess. So much money is spent on what people *want*, while so many people are in *need*. May I be mindful of those who lack basic necessities. Stir in me the needed motivation to contribute to their well being, not just out of my excess, but in a way that requires a sacrifice and that reflects all that you have given me.

ADVENT ACTION

Give of your time, talent, and treasure to those in need. Volunteer time for a social service agency or make a charitable donation, perhaps to Catholic Social Services or a crisis pregnancy center. This is very simple to do on line. The hard part is to move from *thinking* about the donation to actually *making* the donation.

DAY 15

The Dignity of Work

*A*nd *I worked with* my *hands*, and I still desire to work; Acts 20:34 and I earnestly desire all brothers to give themselves to honest work. Let those who do not know how to work learn, not from desire to receive wages, but for an example and to avoid idleness.

SAINT FRANCIS OF ASSISI,
"THE TESTAMENT," 125-126

GROWING THROUGH THE EXPERIENCES OF LIFE

When they [the Holy Family] had finished everything required by the law of the Lord [in the temple in Jerusalem], they returned to Galilee, to their own town of Nazareth. The child grew and became strong, filled with wisdom; and the favor of God was upon him.

LUKE 2:39-40

PRAYER

Jesus, the Scriptures tell us that your stepfather, Joseph, was a carpenter. You know what it is like to toil and labor, and you also know all the benefits of work: learning, growth, and expression of creativity. Help me also to remember the great dignity of work, which is a participation in God's very own ongoing act of creation.

ADVENT ACTION

As you work today, consciously remember that Christ can identify with the challenges that you are facing. In a special way, take pride in your work today.

Boasting in Weakness

*I*n what, then, can you boast? Even if you were so skillful and wise that you possessed *all knowledge*, knew how to interpret every *kind of language*, and to scrutinize heavenly matters with skill: you could not boast in these things. ...In the same way, even if you were more handsome and richer than everyone else, and even if you worked miracles so that you put demons to flight: all these things are contrary to you; nothing belongs to you; you can boast in none of these things.

But we can boast *in* our *weaknesses* and in carrying each day the holy cross of our Lord Jesus Christ.

1 Cor 13:2

1 Cor 12:28

SAINT FRANCIS OF ASSISI, *THE ADMONITIONS*
(V: LET NO ONE BE PROUD,
BUT BOAST IN THE CROSS OF THE LORD), 131

THE POWER OF CHRIST REVEALED IN OUR WEAKNESS

...[The Lord] said to me, "My grace is sufficient for you, for power is made perfect in weakness." So, I will boast all the more gladly of my weaknesses, so that the power of Christ may dwell in me. Therefore I am content with weaknesses, insults, hardships, persecutions, and calamities for the sake of Christ; for whenever I am weak, then I am strong.

2 CORINTHIANS 12:9-10

PRAYER

Lord, any trait or skill is a gift from you and not something of my making. Should I take an unhealthy level of pride in my strengths, this could only lead me away from recognizing my need for you. You demonstrated your own greatness in a most unexpected and yet extraordinary way by becoming a vulnerable infant. Help me to accept and appreciate my weaknesses, for they are what really allow your power and goodness to shine through me.

ADVENT ACTION

Write down two of your weaknesses. Reflect on how God uses these weaknesses to draw you closer to himself and let his own glory be known.

What Is Money Worth?

...[W]e should not think of coin or money having any greater usefulness than stones. The devil wants to blind those who desire or consider it better than stones. May we who have left all things, then, be careful of not losing the kingdom of heaven for so little.

If we find coins anywhere, let us pay no more attention to them than to the dust we trample underfoot, for *vanity of vanities and all is vanity.*

Eccl 1:2

SAINT FRANCIS OF ASSISI, *THE EARLIER RULE*
(VIII: LET THE BROTHERS NOT RECEIVE MONEY), 69-70

DETACHMENT FROM MONEY/WEALTH

As he was setting out on a journey, a man ran up and knelt before him, and asked him, "Good Teacher, what must I do to inherit eternal life?" Jesus said to him, "...You know the commandments: "You shall not murder; You shall not commit adultery; You shall not steal; You shall not bear false witness; You shall not defraud; Honor your father and mother.'" He said to him, "Teacher, I have kept all these since my youth." Jesus, looking at him, loved him and said, "You lack one thing; go, sell what you own, and give the money to the poor, and you will have treasure in heaven; then come, follow me." When he heard this, he was shocked and went away grieving, for he had many possessions. Then Jesus looked around and said to his disciples, "How hard it will be for those who have wealth to enter the kingdom of God!"

MARK 10:17-23

PRAYER

Lord, sometimes it seems as if money can become like a drug. Many people would do almost anything to acquire more money, even if it means harming others. Having heard Francis' warning, may I never let the love of money become an obstacle to my relationship with you. The accumulation of money can never buy the happiness and satisfaction that you alone can give.

ADVENT ACTIVITY

Is the accumulation of money the driving force in your life? Does money serve you, or are you a slave to money? This Advent, practice detachment from money by giving to others without any expectation of repayment. Participate in a free activity that will bring you genuine joy, such as taking a child to a park, visiting or calling a friend, or practicing a random act of kindness.

DAY 18

Difficult People

I speak to you, as best I can, about the state of your soul. You must consider as grace all that impedes you from loving the Lord God and whoever has become an impediment to you, whether brothers or others. ...And may you want it to be this way and not otherwise. And let this be for you the true obedience of the Lord God and my true obedience, for I know with certitude that it is true obedience. And love those who do those things to you and do not wish anything different from them, unless it is something the Lord God shall have given you. And love them in this and do not wish that they were better Christians.

SAINT FRANCIS OF ASSISI,
"A LETTER TO A MINISTER," 97

LOVING EVEN WHEN IT IS DIFFICULT

"You have heard that it was said, 'You shall love your neighbor and hate your enemy.' But I say to you, Love your enemies and pray for those who persecute you, so that you may be sons of your Father who is in heaven; for he makes his sun rise on the evil and on the good, and sends rain on the just and on the unjust. For if you love those who love you, what reward have you? Do not even the tax collectors do the same? And if you salute only your brethren, what more are you doing than others? Do not even the Gentiles do the same? You, therefore, must be perfect, as your heavenly Father is perfect.

MATTHEW 5:43-48

PRAYER

Lord, there are some people around me who just have the ability to step on my last nerve. This is especially true during Advent when tensions are highest and I tend to be more stressed than usual. May I genuinely want what is best for those whom I might not necessarily like.

ADVENT ACTION

Who is it that gets on your nerves? Give thanks for this person for he or she could be a presence in your life that is helping you to grow in ways that please God. Wish this person well or perform some other act of kindness for this person today.

DAY 19

Loving God for All of His Gifts

With our whole heart,
our whole soul,
our whole mind,
with our whole strength and fortitude

Lk 10:27/
Mk 12:30-33

with our whole understanding
with all our powers
with every effort,
every affection,
every feeling,
every desire and wish

Mk 12:30

let us all love *the Lord God*
Who has given and gives to each one of us
our whole body, our whole soul and our whole life,

Who has created, redeemed and will save us
by His mercy alone, Tb 13:5
Who did and does everything good for us…

SAINT FRANCIS OF ASSISI, *THE EARLIER RULE*
(XXIII: PRAYER AND THANKSGIVING), 84

GREAT IS MY LOVE FOR GOD

I love you, O Lord, my strength.
The Lord is my rock, my fortress, and my deliverer,
my God, my rock in whom I take refuge,
my shield, and the horn of my salvation, my stronghold.

PSALM 18:1-2

PRAYER

God of all goodness, my love for you is only a small reflection of the over-powering love that you have for me. May I always continue to love you with every ounce of my being. This is what you created me for. This is the best gift that I can give you in return for all that you have given me.

ADVENT ACTION

Allow yourself to experience the feelings that well up inside of you when you consider God's love. Why do you love God? Name two ways your love for God affects your life.

DAY 20

Source of All Beauty and Goodness

Ps 77:15   You are the holy Lord God *Who does wonderful things.*

Ps 86:10   You are strong. *You are great.* You are the most high.

Jn17:11   You are the almighty king. You *holy Father,*

Mt 11:25   King of *heaven and earth.*

Ps 136:2   You are three and one, the Lord *God of gods;*
      You are the good, all good, the highest good,

1 Thes 1:19   Lord God *living and true.*

    You are love, charity; You are wisdom, You are humility,

Ps 71:5   *You are patience,* You are beauty, You are meekness,
      You are security, You are rest,
      You are gladness and joy, You are our hope, You are justice,
      You are moderation, You are all our riches to sufficiency.

You are beauty, You are meekness,
You are the protector, You are our custodian and defender, Ps 31:5
You are strength, You are refreshment. You are our hope, Ps 43:2
You are our faith, You are our charity,
You are all our sweetness, You are our eternal life:
Great and wonderful Lord, Almighty God, Merciful Savior.

SAINT FRANCIS OF ASSISI, "THE PRAISES OF GOD," 109*

**Written in Francis's own hand after he had received the stigmata.
The original parchment is in poor condition.
Scholars have had to interpolate the text based on the best reading
of the parchment and early copies of it (FA:ED I 108).*

PRAISING GOD'S SPLENDOR

*Great is the Lord, and greatly to be praised;
his greatness is unsearchable.*

*One generation shall laud your works to another,
and shall declare your mighty acts.
On the glorious splendour of your majesty,
and on your wondrous works, I will meditate.
The might of your awesome deeds shall be proclaimed,
and I will declare your greatness.*

PSALM 145:3-6

PRAYER

God, Advent is a time to rejoice in all the goodness that is and all the goodness that is yet to come. Help me to see the beauty and goodness in things, events, and people, even when such beauty and goodness may not at first be apparent. In discovering such beauty and goodness, I am indeed finding you.

ADVENT ACTION

What do you do when you see a beautiful person, sculpture, or hear a piece of music that moves you? How do you react? Be especially attuned to the beauty and goodness around you today, even when they might be hard to see at first glance. Remember that this beauty and goodness is a revelation of God's own self.

DAY 21

Accepting Correction

*B*lessed is the servant who endures discipline, accusation, and reprimand from another as patiently as he would from himself.

Blessed in the servant who, after being reprimanded, agrees courteously, submits respectfully, admits humbly, and makes amends willingly.

Blessed is the servant who is not quick to excuse himself, and endures with humility, shame, and reprimand for a sin, when he did not commit the fault.

SAINT FRANCIS OF ASSISI, *THE ADMONITIONS*
(XXII: CORRECTION), 135

Growing and Learning from Mistakes

Poverty and disgrace are for the one who ignores instruction,
but one who heeds reproof is honored.

Proverbs 13:18

Those who ignore instruction despise themselves,
but those who heed admonition gain understanding.

Proverbs 15:32

Prayer

Lord, open my mind and heart so that I might grow from the wisdom that others have to offer me. This Advent, may I respond positively, rather than defensively, to the correction pointed out by others, so that such correction might make me a better disciple of yours.

Advent Action

When someone else corrects you today, rather than becoming defensive, smile and thank him or her for the direction and advice. Whether the correction is justified or not, consider how it could be used to help you grow into a better person.

Christmas Bells Are Ringing

*M*ay you announce and preach His praise to all nations in such a way that praise and thanks may always be given to the all-powerful God by all people throughout the world at every hour and whenever bells are rung.

SAINT FRANCIS OF ASSISI,
"FIRST LETTER TO THE CUSTODIANS," 57

PRAISING GOD WITH MUSICAL SOUND

Praise the Lord!
Praise God in his sanctuary;
*   praise him in his mighty firmament!*
Praise him for his mighty deeds;
praise him according to his surpassing greatness!

Praise him with trumpet sound;
*   praise him with lute and harp!*
Praise him with tambourine and dance;
*   praise him with strings and pipe!*
Praise him with clanging cymbals;
*   praise him with loud clashing cymbals!*
Let everything that breathes praise the Lord!
Praise the Lord!

PSALM 150:1-6

PRAYER

Lord, the melodic ringing of bells stirs me with excitement; let the ringing of bells bring me joy.

ADVENT ACTION

Use a bell as a call to personal or family prayer today. Offer up a short prayer of praise and thanksgiving when you hear a bell of any type (including bells in songs).

Reverence for Word and Sacrament

*B*ecause *whoever belongs to God hears the words of God,* we Jn 8:47
...must not only listen to and do what the Lord says but
also care for the vessels and other liturgical objects that contain
His holy words in order to impress on ourselves the sublimity
of our Creator and our subjection to Him. I, therefore, admonish all my brothers and encourage them in Christ to venerate,
as best they can, the divine written words wherever they find
them. If they are not well kept or are carelessly thrown around
in some place, let them gather them up and preserve them,
inasmuch as it concerns them, honoring in the words the Lord
Who spoke them. For many things are made holy by the words 3 Kgs 2:4
of God and the sacrament of the altar is celebrated in the power 1 Tm 4:5
of the words of Christ.

SAINT FRANCIS OF ASSISI,
"A LETTER TO THE ENTIRE ORDER," 119

LIVING ON THE WORD OF GOD

Then Jesus was led up by the Spirit into the wilderness to be tempted by the devil. He fasted forty days and forty nights, and afterwards he was famished. The tempter came and said to him, "If you are the Son of God, command these stones to become loaves of bread." But he answered, "It is written,
'One does not live by bread alone,
but by every word that comes from the mouth of God.' "

MATTHEW 4:1-4

PRAYER

Word Made Flesh, may I follow Francis' exhortation and come to greater reverence for your presence, both in word and in sacrament. Help me always to remember that it is not things of the world that will feed my deepest hungers, but only the nourishment that you give me.

ADVENT ACTION

Read from the Scriptures (perhaps Colossians 3:16-17) as part of your prayer before a meal or at bedtime. Place your Bible in a place worthy of its dignity where it is easily accessible in your household.

DAY 24

Setting Aside Cares and Worries

...[I]n the holy love which is God, I beg all my brothers...after 1 Jn 4:16
overcoming every impediment and putting aside every care and
anxiety, to serve, love, honor and adore the Lord God with a
clean heart and a pure mind in whatever way they are best able
to do so, for that is what He wants above all else.

SAINT FRANCIS OF ASSISI, *THE EARLIER RULE*
(XXII: AN ADMONITION TO THE BROTHERS), 80

Letting Go and Letting God

"Therefore I tell you, do not be anxious about your life, what you shall eat or what you shall drink, nor about your body, what you will wear. Is not life more than food, and the body more than clothing? Look at the birds of the air; they neither sow nor reap nor gather into barns, and yet your heavenly Father feeds them. Are you not of more value than they? And can any of you by worrying add a single hour to your span of life? …"So do not be worry about tomorrow, for tomorrow will bring worries of its own. Today's trouble is enough for today.

MATTHEW 6:25-27, 34

Prayer

Lord, there are enough cares and worries to consume me during any other time of year, but these cares and worries seem to multiply during this season. Remind me that my life is in your hands. In doing so, I seek to follow the example of Francis and to better serve and love you.

Advent Action

Is there a worry or concern that is weighing heavy on your mind today? Write it on a piece of paper and entrust it to the Christ-child in the manger.

DAY 25

Unconditional Love

*B*lessed is the servant who loves his brother as much when he is sick and cannot repay him as when he is well and can repay him.

Blessed is the servant who loves and respects his brother as much when he is far away from him as when he is with him, and who would not say anything behind his back that he would not say with charity in his presence.

SAINT FRANCIS OF ASSISI, *THE ADMONITIONS*
(XXIV: TRUE LOVE AND XXV: THE SAME POINT), 136

LOVING GOD BY LOVING OTHERS

We love because he first loved us. Those who say, "I love God," and hate their brothers or sisters, are liars; for those who do not love a brother or sister whom they have seen, cannot love God whom they have not seen. The commandment we have from him is this: those who love God must love their brothers and sisters also.

1 JOHN 4:19-21

PRAYER

Lord, through your own life, you demonstrated the meaning of unconditional love by accepting your disciples with all of their weaknesses and faults. May all Christians put your example into practice and build the kingdom in the world today.

ADVENT ACTION

If someone wrongs or displeases you today, consciously find it in your heart to love that person in spite of his or her faults. Let that person know that you love him or her unconditionally, either verbally, by performing an act of kindness, or simply by overlooking the wrong that has been done.

DAY 26

God Alone Suffices (The Perfect Gift)

Therefore,
let us desire nothing else,
let us want nothing else,
let nothing else please us and cause us delight
except our Creator, Redeemer and Savior,
the only true God,
Who is full of good,
all good, every good, the true and supreme good,
Who alone is good,   Lk 18:19
merciful, gentle, delightful, and sweet,
Who alone is holy,
just, true, holy, and upright,
Who alone is kind, innocent, clean,
From Whom, *through Whom* and in Whom   Heb 2:10
is all pardon, all grace, all glory

of all penitents and just ones,
of all blessed rejoicing together in heaven.

Therefore,
let nothing hinder us,
nothing separate us,
nothing come between us.

SAINT FRANCIS OF ASSISI, *THE EARLIER RULE*
(XIII: PRAYER AND THANKSGIVING), 85

ALL THAT I WANT AND NEED

One thing I asked of the Lord,
   that will I seek after:
to live in the house of the Lord
   all the days of my life,
to behold the beauty of the Lord,
   and to inquire in his temple.

For he will hide me in his shelter
   in the day of trouble;
he will conceal me under the cover of his tent;
   he will set me high on a rock.

Now my head is lifted up
   above my enemies all around me,
and I will offer in his tent
   sacrifices with shouts of joy;
I will sing and make melody to the Lord.

PSALM 27:4-6

PRAYER

In this season, I exhaust myself trying to find the perfect gifts for others. I am also half-convinced that I will only be satisfied if I receive the perfect gift. However, you are the perfect gift; you alone bring satisfaction and fulfillment in my life. All others things leave me feeling empty. This Advent, you alone suffice to bring happiness and peace in my life.

ADVENT ACTION

Focus on the real meaning of Christmas and discuss with family and friends ways of reducing its commercial aspect. When compelled to make an impulse purchase, stop yourself and think of the real reason why you want to make the purchase.

DAY 27

A Loving Faith in Action

*L*et them [the brothers] love one another, as the Lord says: *This is my commandment: love one another as I have loved* Jn 15:12 *you.* Let them express the love they have for one another by their deeds, as the Apostle says: *Let us not love in word or speech, but* 1 Jn 3:18 *in deed and truth.*

SAINT FRANCIS OF ASSISI, *THE EARLIER RULE*
(XI: THE BROTHERS SHOULD NOT REVILE OR DETRACT,
BUT SHOULD LOVE ONE ANOTHER), 72

Let all the brothers ... preach by their deeds.

SAINT FRANCIS OF ASSISI, *THE EARLIER RULE*
(XVII: PREACHERS), 75

LET YOUR LIGHT SHINE

"You are the salt of the earth; but if salt has lost its taste, how can its saltiness be restored? It is no longer good for anything, but is thrown out and trampled under foot. "You are the light of the world. A city built on a hill cannot be hid. No one after lighting a lamp puts it under the bushel basket, but on the lampstand, and it gives light to all in the house. In the same way, let your light shine before others, so that they may see your good works and give glory to your Father in heaven.

MATTHEW 5:13-16

PRAYER

Lord, you command me to love my neighbor, and you ask me to spread the Good News about your deep love for all people. May I put this love in practice.

ADVENT ACTION

Demonstrate your genuine love for others by putting aside your own desires in order to serve someone else. For example, set aside personal time to visit or send several Christmas cards to a shut-in or someone with whom you have lost contact in your life.

DAY 28

Human Humility

1 Jn 4:16 *I*n the love that is God, therefore, I beg all my brothers—those who preach, pray, or work, cleric or lay—to strive to humble themselves in everything, not to boast or delight in themselves or inwardly exalt themselves because of the good words and deeds or, for that matter, because of any good that God sometimes says or does or works in and through them... We may know with certainty that nothing belongs to us except our vices and our sins.

SAINT FRANCIS OF ASSISI, *THE EARLIER RULE*
(XVII: PREACHERS), 75

Mt 24:46 *Blessed is that servant* who no more exalts himself over the good the Lord says or does through him than over what He says or does through another.

A person sins who wishes to receive more from his neighbor than what he wishes to give of himself to the Lord.

SAINT FRANCIS OF ASSISI, *THE ADMONITIONS* (XVII: THE HUMBLE SERVANT OF GOD), 134

BECOMING THE SERVANT OF OTHERS

Then they came to Capernaum; and when he was in the house he asked them, "What were you arguing about on the way?" But they were silent, for on the way they had argued with one another who was the greatest. He sat down, called the twelve, and said to them, "Whoever wants to be first must be last of all and servant of all." Then he took a little child and put it among them; and taking it in his arms, he said to them, "Whoever welcomes one such child in my name welcomes me, and whoever welcomes me welcomes not me but the one who sent me."

MARK 9:33-37

PRAYER

Help me to remember that all that is good is a gift from you, as is everything. Help me to remember also that you came to serve, not to be served. May I reach out to others in love by modeling my own life on that of your humble servant, Francis, who laid down his life in service of others.

ADVENT ACTION

Perform a humble act of service today. Be spontaneous as to when and where you choose to do it.

PART II

Readings
for the
Christmas
Season

DAY 1

Shout to the Lord Because
the Savior Is Born!

Ps 81:2 *Exult in God our help!*

Ps 47:2   Shout to the Lord God living and true *with cries of gladness!*
Because the Lord, the Most High,

Ps 47:3   *the Awesome, is the Great King over all the earth.*

Ps 74:12 Because the Most Holy Father of heaven, *our King before all ages,*
sent His Beloved Son from on high
and He was born of the Blessed Virgin Holy Mary.

Ps 89:27 *He called to me: You are my Father*
and I will place Him, my firstborn, as the Highest,

Ps 89:28   *above all the kings of the earth.*
On that day the Lord sent His mercy

Ps 42:9   *and at night His song.*
This is the day the Lord has made

Ps 118:24   *let us rejoice and be glad in it.*

For the Most Holy Child has been given to us
and has been born for us on the way Is 9:6
and placed in a manger Lk 2:7
because he did not have a place in the inn.
Glory to the Lord God in the highest
and peace on earth to those of good will. Lk 2:14
Let the heavens rejoice and the earth exult,
let the sea and its fullness resound,
let the fields and all that is in them be joyful. Ps 96:11-12
Sing a new song to the Lord,
sing to the Lord all the earth. Ps 96:1
Because the Lord is great and worth of praise
He is awesome beyond all gods. Ps 96:4
Give to the Lord, you families of nations,
give to the Lord glory and praise,
give to the Lord the glory due His name. Ps 96:7-8
Take up your bodies and carry His holy cross Lk 14:27;
Jn 19:17
And follow His most holy commands even to the end. 1 Pt 2:21

SAINT FRANCIS OF ASSISI, "VESPERS OF THE LORD'S BIRTH,
ANTIPHON: HOLY VIRGIN MARY (PSALM XV)," 156-7*

*Psalms arranged by Saint Francis with interpolations.

GOD'S SON HAS BEEN GIVEN TO US

For a child has been born for us,
a son given to us;
authority rests upon his shoulders;
and he is named Wonderful Counselor, Mighty God,
Everlasting Father, Prince of Peace.
His authority shall grow continually,

and there shall be endless peace
for the throne of David and his kingdom.
He will establish and uphold it
with justice and with righteousness
from this time onward and forevermore.
The zeal of the Lord of hosts will do this.

ISAIAH 9:6-7

PRAYER

The wondrous gift has been given! Let the celebration begin! God has chosen to dwell among us. Lord Jesus, thank you for coming into our world and joining in our human condition. You have humbled yourself in order to give yourself to us, to join with us as intimately as possible. Joined with all creation, our hearts cannot help but shout with joy!

CHRISTMAS ACTION

Sit before a nativity scene. Meditate on the scene and place yourself in it. Where would you stand? What would you feel? Picture yourself holding the infant Jesus in your arms. What would you say to him? Say it to him in your heart.

Emulating the Lives of the Saints:
Walking the Walk vs. Talking the Talk

*T*he Lord's sheep followed Him in tribulation and persecution, in shame and hunger, in weakness and temptation, and in other ways; and for these things they received eternal life from the Lord.

Therefore, it is a shame for us, the servants of God, that the saints have accomplished great things and we want only to receive glory and honor by recounting them.

SAINT FRANCIS OF ASSISI, *THE ADMONITIONS*
(VI: IMITATION OF CHRIST), 131

The Witness of the First Martyr

Stephen, full of grace and power, did great wonders and signs among the people. Then some of those who belonged to the synagogue of the Freedmen (as it was called)…stood up and argued with Stephen. But they could not withstand the wisdom and the Spirit with which he spoke. …When they heard these things, they became enraged and ground their teeth at Stephen. But filled with the Holy Spirit, he gazed into heaven and saw the glory of God and Jesus standing at the right hand of God. "Look," he said, "I see the heavens opened and the Son of Man standing at the right hand of God!" But they covered their ears, and with a loud shout all rushed together against him. Then they dragged him out of the city and began to stone him; and the witnesses laid their coats at the feet of a young man named Saul. While they were stoning Stephen, he prayed, "Lord Jesus, receive my spirit." Then he knelt down and cried out in a loud voice, "Lord, do not hold this sin against them." When he had said this, he died.

ACTS 6:8-10; 7:54-60

Prayer

Lord, as Francis admonishes, let me not only recount the lives of the saints, but also seek to imitate their courageous example.

CHRISTMAS ACTION

When tempted to take the easy way out of a situation in which your Christian calling demands that you step up and say or do something, turn to Christ for courage, take the more difficult but more rewarding way of the saints, and do the right thing.

The Love of God in the Incarnation

We thank You
for as through Your Son You created us,
so through Your holy love
with which You love us
You brought about His birth
as true God and true man
by the glorious, ever-virgin, most blessed, holy Mary
and You willed to redeem us captives
through His cross and blood and death.

Jn 17:26

SAINT FRANCIS OF ASSISI, *THE EARLIER RULE*
(XXIII: PRAYER AND THANKSGIVING), 82

THE GREAT EXPRESSION OF THE FATHER'S LOVE

"For God so loved the world that he gave his only Son, so that everyone who believes in him may not perish but may have eternal life.

"Indeed, God did not send the Son into the world to condemn the world, but in order that the world might be saved through him. ..."

JOHN 3:16-17

PRAYER

God of all compassion, you loved your people so much that you could not help but share yourself with us by taking on human flesh. A greater outpouring of love the world has never seen. A greater gift there has never been than the message of the depths of your love for all people as found in the birth of Jesus Christ.

CHRISTMAS ACTION

If possible, take ten minutes today and call or write a note to someone you know who is having a difficult time coping with a situation.

DAY 4

Creation's Song of Praise

Most High, all-powerful, good Lord,

Rv 4:9, 11   Yours are *the praises, the glory,* and *the honor,* and all *blessing,*
To You alone, Most High, do they belong,
    and no human is worthy to mention Your name.

Tb 8:7   Praised be You, my *Lord,* with all *Your creatures,*
    especially Sir Brother Sun,
    Who is the day and through whom You give us light.
And he is beautiful and radiant with great splendor;
    and bears a likeness to You, Most High One.

Ps 148:3   *Praised* be You, my Lord, through Sister *Moon* and *the stars,*
    in heaven You formed them clear and precious and beautiful.
Praised be You, my Lord, through Brother Wind,
    and through the air, cloudy and serene,
    and every kind of weather,
    through whom you give sustenance to Your creatures.

Praised be You, my Lord, through Sister *Water,*   Ps 148:4,5
   who is very useful and humble and precious and chaste.
Praised be You, my Lord, through Brother *Fire,*   Dn 3:66
   through whom *You light the night,*   Ps 78:14
   and he is beautiful and playful and robust and strong.
Praised be You, my Lord , through our Sister Mother *Earth,*   Dn 3:74
   who sustains and governs us,
   and who produces various *fruit* with colored flowers
   and *herbs.*   Ps 104:13,14

Praised be You, my Lord, through those who give pardon
   for Your love,   Mt 6:12
   and bear infirmity and tribulation.
      Blessed are those who endure in peace
      for by You, Most High, shall they be crowned.

Praised be You, my Lord, through our Sister Bodily Death,
   from whom no one living can escape.
   Woe to those who die in mortal sin.
   Blessed are those whom death will find in
   Your most holy will,
   for *the second death* shall do them no harm.   Rv 2:11; 20:6

Praise and *bless* my *Lord* and give Him thanks   Dn 3:85
   and serve Him with great humility.

SAINT FRANCIS OF ASSISI,
"CANTICLE OF CREATURES," 113-114

CREATION REJOICES IN THE CREATOR

The pastures of the wilderness overflow,
the hills gird themselves with joy,
the meadows clothe themselves with flocks,
the valleys deck themselves with grain,
they shout and sing together for joy.

PSALM 65:12-13

PRAYER

God of all creation, all of your works join me in giving praise to you. Like Francis, may I always be aware of the ways you reveal yourself through things great and small.

CHRISTMAS ACTION

Francis refers to the weather as our brother and sister. How do the seasons mirror the cycles in your own life? Where, during this winter, can you find life and give life?

:::: DAY 5 :::

Being Christ's Relatives

*W*e are spouses [of Christ] when the faithful soul is joined by the Holy Spirit to our Lord Jesus Christ. We are brothers to Him when we do *the will of the Father who is in heaven.* We are mothers when we carry Him in our heart and body through divine love and a pure and sincere conscience and give birth to Him through a holy activity which must shine as an example before others.

Mt 12:50

1 Cor 6:20

Mt 5:16

SAINT FRANCIS OF ASSISI, *EARLY EXHORTATION*
TO THE BROTHERS AND SISTERS OF PENANCE
(I: THOSE WHO DO PENANCE), 42

ACTING ON THE WORD TO BECOME CHRIST'S FAMILY

But he [Jesus] said to them, "My mother and my brothers are those who hear the word of God and do it."

LUKE 8:21

PRAYER

Newborn Christ-child, may I always carry you in my heart and bring you to others through my loving actions. Let all that I do, all that I say, and all that I think deepen in this season.

CHRISTMAS ACTION

How will you make more time for your relationship with Christ in the New Year?

Peace

*B*lessed are the peacemakers, for they will be called children *of God.*

Mt 5:9

Those people are truly peacemakers who, regardless of what they suffer in this world, preserve peace of spirit and body out of love of our Lord Jesus Christ.

SAINT FRANCIS, *THE ADMONITIONS* (XV: PEACE), 134

And when we are not paid for our work, let us have recourse to the table of the Lord, begging alms from door to door. The Lord revealed a greeting to me that we should say: *"May the Lord give you peace."*

SAINT FRANCIS OF ASSISI, "THE TESTAMENT," 125-126

THE REIGN OF CHRIST'S PEACE

A shoot shall come out from the stock of Jesse,
and a branch shall grow out of his roots.
The spirit of the Lord shall rest on him,
the spirit of wisdom and understanding,
the spirit of counsel and might,
the spirit of knowledge and the fear of the Lord.
Righteousness shall be the belt around his waist,
and faithfulness the belt around his loins.
The wolf shall live with the lamb,
the leopard shall lie down with the kid,
the calf and the lion and the fatling together,
and a little child shall lead them.
The cow and the bear shall graze,
their young shall lie down together;
and the lion shall eat straw like the ox.
The nursing child shall play over the hole of the asp,
and the weaned child shall put its hand
on the adder's den.

ISAIAH 11:1-2, 5-8

GOD'S CHILDREN

"Blessed are the peacemakers,
for they will be called children of God."

MATTHEW 5:9

PRAYER

Prince of Peace, you joined us in our humanity, not as a mighty warrior but as an innocent baby. You came to teach us the way to lasting peace. Lead all of us in finding peaceful resolutions to conflicts in our cities, our nation, and our world. Grant us the peace that only you can give.

CHRISTMAS ACTION

The roots of conflict are many: poverty, injustice, lack of education, cultural misunderstandings. How does your faith influence you to be an active agent in the fight against these issues, or does it?

DAY 7

Following In Christ's Footsteps

Almighty, eternal, just and merciful God,
give us miserable ones
the grace to do for You alone
what we know you want us to do
and always to desire what pleases You.
Inwardly cleansed,
interiorly enlightened
and inflamed by the fire of the Holy Spirit,
May we be able to follow
in the footsteps of Your beloved Son,
our Lord Jesus Christ
and, by Your grace alone,
may we make our way to You,

Most High,
Who live and rule
in perfect Trinity and simple Unity,
and are glorified
God almighty,
forever and ever.
Amen.

SAINT FRANCIS OF ASSISI,
"A LETTER TO THE ENTIRE ORDER (PRAYER)," 120-121

FOLLOWING THE WAY OF THE MASTER

Those who love their life lose it, and those who hate their life in this world will keep it for eternal life. Whoever serves me must follow me, and where I am, there will my servant be also. Whoever serves me, the Father will honor.

JOHN 12:25-26

PRAYER

Lord Jesus, you stumbled before you walked, but your steps became sure as you matured and set out to follow your Father's will. Lead by the hand all the men and women who have promised to follow you.

CHRISTMAS ACTION

For ten minutes, sit quietly and meditate on the words of the "Our Father." Let the prayer become one with your breath so that the words work deep into your soul.

Mary: Queen, Intercessor, and Model of Christian Discipleship

Holy Virgin Mary,
among the women born into the world,
there is no one like you.
Daughter and servant
of the most high and supreme king
and of the Father in heaven,
Mother of our most holy Lord Jesus Christ,
Spouse of the Holy Spirit,
pray for us
with Saint Michael the Archangel,
all the powers of heaven
and all the saints,

at the side of your most holy beloved Son,
our Lord and Teacher.

SAINT FRANCIS OF ASSISI,
"MARIAN ANTIPHON: HOLY VIRGIN MARY," 141

FAITHFUL MOTHER, FAITHFUL DISCIPLE

*On the third day there was a wedding in Cana of Galilee,
and the mother of Jesus was there. Jesus and his disciples had
also been invited to the wedding. When the wine gave out,
the mother of Jesus said to him, "They have no wine." And
Jesus said to her, "Woman, what concern is that to you and
to me? My hour has not yet come." His mother said to the
servants, "Do whatever he tells you."*

JOHN 2:1-5

PRAYER

Mary, God became present in the world through you. You
were God's instrument. May God's presence shine in the
world through my life.

CHRISTMAS ACTION

On this, the Solemnity of Mary, Mother of God, use the
mysteries of the rosary to guide your reflection. Consider
the ways in which Mary was a faithful disciple of Christ.

DAY 9

Seeing through God's Eyes

*K*now that there are certain very lofty and sublime things in the sight of God that people sometimes think of as worthless and contemptible; there are others that are esteemed and remarkable to people that God considers extremely worthless and contemptible.

SAINT FRANCIS OF ASSISI,
"THE SECOND LETTER TO THE CUSTODIANS," 60

Rejecting the Values of Contemporary Society

Do not love the world or the things in the world. The love of the Father is not in those who love the world; for all that is in the world—the desire of the flesh, the desire of the eyes, the pride in riches—comes not from the Father but from the world. And the world and its desire are passing away, but those who do the will of God live forever.

1 JOHN 2:15-17

Prayer

Lord, your birth showed that your ways often contradict the typical thinking of the world. Help us value that which you value and to reject that which is contrary to your will, even though the world might tell us otherwise.

Christmas Action

Write down your top five priorities in life. Be honest. Do they reflect what is really most important in life from God's point of view? Are your priorities in proper order? Could you explain why to someone else?

Opening Ourselves to the Humility
of Christ in the Eucharist

Let everyone be struck with fear,
let the whole world tremble,
and let the heavens exalt
when Christ the Son of the living God,
is present on the altar in the hands of a priest!
O wonderful loftiness and stupendous dignity!
O sublime humility!
O humble sublimity!
The Lord of the universe,
God and the Son of God,
so humbles Himself
that for our salvation
He hides Himself
under an ordinary piece of bread!

Brothers, look at the humility of God,
and *pour our your hearts before Him*! Ps 62:9
Humble yourselves
that you may be exalted by Him! 1 Pt 5:6;
Jas 4:10
Hold back nothing of yourselves for yourselves,
that He Who gives Himself totally to you
may receive you totally!

SAINT FRANCIS OF ASSISI,
"A LETTER TO THE ENTIRE ORDER," 118

TRUE LIFE IN CHRIST

Abide in me as I abide in you. Just as the branch cannot bear fruit by itself unless it abides in the vine, neither can you unless you abide in me. I am the vine, you are the branches. Those who abide in me and I in them bear much fruit, because apart from me you can do nothing.

JOHN 15:4-5

PRAYER

Lord Jesus, through the Eucharist, lead me to the true life that is found in giving of myself for others as you gave of yourself for all humankind.

CHRISTMAS ACTION

If you can, attend Mass today or spend time in the presence of Christ in the Eucharist. Practice a form of self-emptying by eating less than you ordinarily would or by passing up a snack. What would life be like if you were unable to go to Mass and receive the Eucharist?

Finding God in the Poor and Marginalized

They [the brothers] must rejoice when they live among people considered of little value and looked down upon, among the poor and powerless, the sick and lepers, and the beggars by the wayside.

SAINT FRANCIS OF ASSISI, *THE EARLIER RULE*
(IX: BEGGING ALMS), 70

The Lord gave me, Brother Francis, thus to begin doing penance in this way: for when I was in sin, it seemed too bitter for me to see lepers. And the Lord Himself led me among them and *I showed mercy* to them. And when I left them, what had seemed bitter to me was turned into sweetness in soul and body. ...

Sir 35:4

SAINT FRANCIS OF ASSISI, "THE TESTAMENT," 124

THE MESSAGE OF CHRIST'S BIRTH IS
ENTRUSTED TO THE LOWLY

In that region there were shepherds living in the fields, keeping watch over their flock by night. Then an angel of the Lord stood before them, and the glory of the Lord shone around them, and they were terrified. But the angel said to them, "Do not be afraid; for see—I am bringing you good news of great joy for all the people: to you is born this day in the city of David a Savior, who is the Messiah, the Lord. This will be a sign for you: you will find a child wrapped in bands of cloth and lying in a manger." …When the angels had left them and gone into heaven, the shepherds said to one another, "Let us go now to Bethlehem and see this thing that has taken place, which the Lord has made known to us." So they went with haste and found Mary and Joseph, and the child lying in the manger. When they saw this, they made known what had been told them about this child; and all who heard it were amazed at what the shepherds told them.

LUKE 2:8-12, 15-18

PRAYER

Lord Jesus, from the moment of your birth, you identified yourself with the poor and marginalized. It is among the outcasts, despised, and downtrodden that we encounter you today. May we have a special concern for the poor and a desire to reach out to those who are often excluded in our society; help us to see your face in theirs.

CHRISTMAS ACTION

Who are the marginalized in your parish or community? Whom do people avoid? Today, take a specific action to reach out to someone who might otherwise be excluded from a given situation.

DAY 12

Living in Joy

*L*et them [the brothers] be careful not to appear outwardly
as sad and gloomy hypocrites but show themselves *joyful,*
cheerful and consistently gracious *in the Lord.*   Phil 4:4

SAINT FRANCIS OF ASSISI, *THE EARLIER RULE*
(VII: THE MANNER OF SERVING AND WORKING), 69

THE JOY OF THE STAR

When they had heard the king, they set out; and there, ahead of them, went the star that they had seen at its rising, until it stopped over the place where the child was. When they saw that the star had stopped, they were overwhelmed with joy. On entering the house, they saw the child with Mary his mother; and they knelt down and paid him homage. Then, opening their treasure chests, they offered him gifts of gold, frankincense, and myrrh.

MATTHEW 2:9-11

PRAYER

Lord God, many Christians go through the world disheartened and dejected. Through your grace, stir in them the confidence to embrace your strength that prevails in the darkest moments of life, so that when feeling dejected, they may see our support and care.

CHRISTMAS ACTION

Our society is racially diverse, and consequently, so is the Church. In a spirit of openness, attend a parish function or liturgy where you will meet and pray with others who share core Christian beliefs, but who may express them in a different language and with different music.

PART III

~~~~~~~~

Formats for Nightly Prayer and Reading

Formats for
Nightly Prayer and Reading

THE PURPOSE OF PRESENTING these two optional formats for nightly readings and prayer is to offer different ways to use the material in this book for group or individual prayer. Of course, there are other ways in which to use this book—for example, as a meditative daily reader or as a guide for a prayer journal—but the following familiar liturgical formats provide a structure that can be used in a variety of contexts.

FORMAT 1

OPENING PRAYER

The observance begins with these words:

God, come to my assistance.
Lord, make haste to help me.

followed by:

Glory to the Father, and to the Son,
and to the Holy Spirit, as it was in the beginning,
is now, and will be for ever. Amen. Alleluia.

EXAMINATION OF CONSCIENCE

If this observance is being prayed individually, an examination of conscience may be included. Here is a short examination of conscience; you may, of course, use your own preferred method.

1. Place yourself in a quiet frame of mind.
2. Review your life since your last confession.
3. Reflect on the Ten Commandments and any sins against these commandments.
4. Reflect on the words of the gospel, especially Jesus' commandment to love your neighbor as yourself.
5. Ask yourself these questions: How have I been unkind in thoughts, words, and actions? Am I refusing to forgive anyone? Do I despise any group or person? Am I a prisoner of fear, anxiety, worry, guilt, inferiority, or hatred of myself?

PENITENTIAL RITE (OPTIONAL)

If a group of people are praying in unison, a penitential rite from the *Roman Missal* may be used:

Presider: Lord Jesus, you came to call all people to yourself: Lord, have mercy.

All: Lord, have mercy.

Presider: Lord Jesus, you come to us in word and prayer: Christ, have mercy.

All: Christ, have mercy.

Presider: Lord Jesus, you will appear in glory with all your saints:
Lord, have mercy.

All: Lord, have mercy.

Presider: May almighty God have mercy on us, forgive us our sins, and bring us to life everlasting.

All: Amen.

HYMN: "O COME, O COME, EMMANUEL"

A hymn is now sung or recited. This Advent hymn is a paraphrase of the great "O" Antiphons written in the twelfth century and translated by John Mason Neale in 1852.

O come, O come, Emmanuel,
And ransom captive Israel;
That mourns in lonely exile here,
Until the Son of God appear.

Refrain: Rejoice! Rejoice! O Israel
　　　　　　To thee shall come, Emmanuel!

O come, thou wisdom, from on high,
And order all things far and nigh;
To us the path of knowledge show,
And teach us in her ways to go.

Refrain

O come, O come, thou Lord of might,
Who to thy tribes on Sinai's height
In ancient times did give the law,
In cloud, and majesty, and awe.

Refrain

O come, thou rod of Jesse's stem,
From ev'ry foe deliver them
That trust thy mighty power to save,
And give them vict'ry o'er the grave.

Refrain

O come, thou key of David, come,
And open wide our heav'nly home,
Make safe the way that leads on high,
That we no more have cause to sigh.

Refrain

O come, thou Dayspring from on high,
And cheer us by thy drawing nigh;
Disperse the gloomy clouds of night
And death's dark shadow put to flight.

Refrain

O come, Desire of nations, bind
In one the hearts of all mankind;
Bid every strife and quarrel cease
And fill the world with heaven's peace.

Refrain

PSALM 27:7–14—GOD STANDS BY US IN DANGERS

Hear, O LORD, when I cry aloud,
    be gracious to me and answer me!
"Come," my heart says, "seek his face!"
    Your face, LORD, do I seek.
    Do not hide your face from me.

Do not turn your servant away in anger,
 you who have been my help.
Do not cast me off, do not forsake me,
 O God of my salvation!
If my father and mother forsake me,
 the LORD will take me up.

Teach me your way, O LORD,
 and lead me on a level path
 because of my enemies.
Do not give me up to the will of my adversaries,
 for false witnesses have risen against me,
 and they are breathing out violence.

I believe that I shall see the goodness of the LORD
 in the land of the living.
Wait for the LORD;
 be strong, and let your heart take courage;
 wait for the LORD!

RESPONSE

I long to see your face, O Lord. You are my light and my help.
Do not turn away from me.

SCRIPTURE READING

Read silently or have a presider proclaim the Scripture of the
day that is selected.

RESPONSE

Come and set us free, Lord God of power and might. Let your face shine on us and we will be saved.

Glory to the Father, and to the Son,
and to the Holy Spirit:
as it was in the beginning, is now,
and will be for ever. Amen.

SECOND READING

Read the excerpt from Saint Francis of Assisi for the day selected.

CANTICLE OF SIMEON

Lord, now you let your servant go in peace;
your word has been fulfilled:
my own eyes have seen the salvation
which you have prepared in the sight of every people:
a light to reveal you to the nations
and the glory of your people Israel.

Glory to the Father, and to the Son, and to the Holy Spirit:
as it was in the beginning, is now,
and will be for ever. Amen.

PRAYER

Say the prayer that follows the day's selected excerpt from Saint Francis of Assisi.

BLESSING

May the all-powerful Lord grant us a restful night and a peaceful death. Amen.

MARIAN ANTIPHON

Loving mother of the Redeemer,
gate of heaven, star of the sea,
assist your people who have fallen yet strive to rise again.
To the wonderment of nature you bore your Creator,
yet remained a virgin after as before.
You who received Gabriel's joyful greeting,
have pity on us poor sinners.

FORMAT 2

OPENING PRAYER

The observance begins with these words:

God, come to my assistance.
Lord, make haste to help me.

followed by:

Glory to the Father, and to the Son,
and to the Holy Spirit, as it was in the beginning,
is now, and will be for ever. Amen. Alleluia.

EXAMINATION OF CONSCIENCE

If this observance is being prayed individually, an examination of conscience may be included. Here is a short examination of conscience; you may, of course, use your own preferred method.

1. Place yourself in a quiet frame of mind.
2. Review your life since your last confession.
3. Reflect on the Ten Commandments and any sins against these commandments.
4. Reflect on the words of the gospel, especially Jesus' commandment to love your neighbor as yourself.
5. Ask yourself these questions: How have I been unkind in thoughts, words, and actions? Am I refusing to forgive anyone? Do I despise any group or person? Am I a prisoner of fear, anxiety, worry, guilt, inferiority, or hatred of myself?

PENITENTIAL RITE (OPTIONAL)

If a group of people are praying in unison, a penitential rite from the *Roman Missal* may be used:

All:
I confess to almighty God,
and to you, my brothers and sisters,
that I have sinned through my own fault
in my thoughts and in my words,
in what I have done,
and in what I have failed to do;
and I ask blessed Mary, ever virgin,
all the angels and saints,
and you, my brothers and sisters,
to pray for me to the Lord our God.

Presider:
May almighty God have mercy on us,
forgive us our sins,
and bring us to life everlasting.

All:
Amen.

Hymn: "Behold, a Rose"

A hymn is now sung or recited. This traditional hymn was composed in German in the fifteenth century. It is sung to the melody of the familiar "Lo, How a Rose E're Blooming."

> Behold, a rose of Judah
> From tender branch has sprung,
> From Jesse's lineage coming,
> As men of old have sung.
> It came a flower bright
> Amid the cold of winter,
> When half spent was the night.
>
> Isaiah has foretold it
> In words of promise sure,
> And Mary's arms enfold it,
> A virgin meek and pure.
> Through God's eternal will
> She bore for men a savior
> At midnight calm and still.

Psalm 40:1–8—Thanksgiving for Deliverance

> I waited patiently for the LORD;
>   he inclined to me and heard my cry.
> He drew me up from the desolate pit,
>   out of the miry bog,
> and set my feet upon a rock,
>   making my steps secure.
> He put a new song in my mouth,
>   a song of praise to our God.

Many will see and fear,
and put their trust in the LORD.

Happy are those who make
the LORD their trust,
who do not turn to the proud,
to those who go astray after false gods.
You have multiplied, O LORD my God,
your wondrous deeds and your thoughts towards us;
none can compare with you.
Were I to proclaim and tell of them,
they would be more than can be counted.

Sacrifice and offering you do not desire,
but you have given me an open ear.
Burnt-offering and sin-offering
you have not required.
Then I said, "Here I am;
in the scroll of the book it is written of me.
I delight to do your will, O my God;
your law is within my heart."

RESPONSE

May all who seek after you be glad in the Lord, may those who find your salvation say with continuous praise, "Great is the Lord!"

SCRIPTURE READING

Read silently or have a presider proclaim the Scripture of the day that is selected.

RESPONSE

Lord, you who were made obedient unto death, teach us to always do the Father's will, so that, sanctified by the holy obedience that joins us to your sacrifice, we can count on your immense love in times of sorrow.

Glory to the Father, and to the Son,
and to the Holy Spirit:
as it was in the beginning, is now,
and will be for ever. Amen.

SECOND READING

Read silently or have a presider read the words of Saint Francis for the day selected.

CANTICLE OF SIMEON

Lord, now you let your servant go in peace;
    your word has been fulfilled:
my own eyes have seen the salvation
    which you have prepared in the sight of every people:
a light to reveal you to the nations
    and the glory of your people Israel.
Glory to the Father, and to the Son,
and to the Holy Spirit:
as it was in the beginning, is now,
and will be for ever. Amen.

PRAYER

Recite the prayer that follows the excerpt from Saint Francis for the day selected.

BLESSING

Lord, give our bodies restful sleep and let the work we have done today bear fruit in eternal life. Watch over us as we rest in your peace. Amen.

MARIAN ANTIPHON

Hail, holy Queen, mother of mercy,
>	our life, our sweetness, and our hope.
To you do we cry,
>	poor banished children of Eve.
To you do we send up our sighs,
>	mourning and weeping in this vale of tears.
Turn then, most gracious advocate,
>	your eyes of mercy toward us,
>	and after this exile
>	show to us the blessed fruit of your womb, Jesus.
O clement, O loving,
O sweet Virgin Mary. Amen.